The Classical Three-Section Staff

THE
CLASSICAL
# Three-Section
# Staff

## RICK L. WING

**BLUE SNAKE BOOKS**
*Berkeley, California*

Published by Blue Snake Books
an imprint of North Atlantic Books
Huichin, unceded Ohlone land
Berkeley, California

Originally published by
Jing Mo Athletic Association
San Francisco, California
www.jingmo.com

Cover and book design by Brad Greene
Printed in the United States of America

*The Classical Three-Section Staff* is sponsored and published by North Atlantic Books, an educational nonprofit based in the unceded Ohlone land Huichin (Berkeley, CA) that collaborates with partners to develop cross-cultural perspectives; nurture holistic views of art, science, the humanities, and healing; and seed personal and global transformation by publishing work on the relationship of body, spirit, and nature.

North Atlantic Books's publications are distributed to the US trade and internationally by Penguin Random House Publisher Services. For further information, visit our website at www.northatlanticbooks.com.

PLEASE NOTE: The creators and publishers of this book are not and will not be responsible, in any way whatsoever, for any improper use made by anyone of the information contained in this book. All use of the aforementioned information must be made in accordance with what is permitted by law, and any damage liable to be caused as a result thereof will be the exclusive responsibility of the user. In addition, they must adhere strictly to the safety rules contained in the book, both in training and in actual implementation of the information presented herein. This book is intended for use in conjunction with ongoing lessons and personal training with an authorized expert. It is not a substitute for formal training. It is the sole responsibility of every person planning to train in the techniques described in this book to consult a licensed physician in order to obtain complete medical information on their personal ability and limitations. The instructions and advice printed in this book are not in any way intended as a substitute for medical, mental, or emotional counseling with a licensed physician or health-care provider.

Library of Congress Cataloging-in-Publication Data

Wing, Rick L.
  The classical three section staff / Rick L. Wing.
    p. cm.
  ISBN 978-1-58394-262-8
  1. Martial arts weapons. 2. Kung fu. I. Title.
  GV1101.5.W57 2008
  796.815'9—dc22                                2008039371


3 4 5 6 7 8 9 10 5LP 29 28 27 26 25 24

This book is dedicated to my instructor,

WONG JACK MAN, SIFU,

my lifelong teacher in the martial tradition.

∿

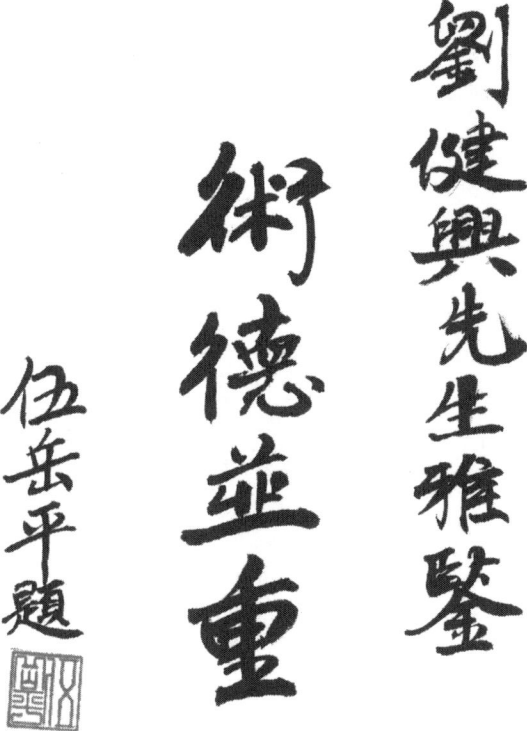

劉健興先生雅鑒

術德並重

伍岳平題

This is presented with gracious respect

to Mr. Rick L. Wing.

Martial ability and virtue, united in one.

SUBMITTED BY SIFU PAUL ENG.

# ACKNOWLEDGMENTS

Ah, again, this is the fun part for me, and my favorite part of the book. The hard work was in the making of the book, but once the work is over, everyone feels better, and we all relax . . . until the next one.

Thanks to Sifu Paul Eng, again and again and again and then . . . one more time. Not only is he a wise man, I really have to say . . . he's cool too, a magnificent blend of traditional wisdom and modern insight. Three guesses as to who did the calligraphy. I'd like to tell you I did, but then . . . that would be an outrageous story . . . even for me. I would also like to thank him for his generous salutation at the beginning of this book. I am deeply honored by it.

Thanks to Stephen Finerty, the desktop computer whiz, who got it together, put it together, and made it look like a real book. Many thanks, Stephen.

Thanks to Albert Koo for his translation skills . . . but honestly I should tell you that, well, actually, he thanked *me* because he said I gave him practice in keeping his Chinese language skills current, but . . . I really think I should thank him, instead of him thanking me. Thanks, Albert.

Thanks to brother Remus Baracca for wielding the spear, and what a spear it was! Around Remus, please, just call me "Romulus." A job well done!

Let us also mention the English teacher, Mr. John Sutherland (from the Scottish Highlands), who has proofread this book to make it socially acceptable to the reading public. His martial expertise, along with his literary expertise, has made this book much better. And in that title of "Mister Sutherland," it has long been rumored that the title should have an "a" instead of an "i." I thank you, and bow humbly and deeply, very deeply, my friend.

Mr. Sutherland's partner in crime, Captain Tom Busby . . . dig it, dig it, dig it, also helped by proofreading this book. Fortunately, or unfortunately, he found even more errors. Thanks for the help, Tom "Pilot" Busby.

Thanks to brother Phillip Wong for taking the photos. He has the routine down, way down. It is his talent that the reader is seeing. When the photos come out good, he gets the credit; when they come out badly, everyone seems to agree that it is 100 percent my fault. He is our resident expert at taking photos, photos, and more photos.

Also, thanks to Erin Wiegand for a guiding hand, to Adrienne Armstrong for triple-checking the words, and to Mr. Jess O'Brien for taking the time.

And once again, special thanks to Sihing Paul Eng for his invaluable assistance.

Lastly, we'd like to thank you, the reader. We hope you enjoy this book!

# TABLE OF CONTENTS

# PREFACE

I learned this form long ago from my gung-fu teacher, Grandmaster Wong Jack Man, a genuine master of the martial arts who was extremely skilled in the use of classical Chinese weaponry. He considered this set to be extremely useful and practical and also a premier demonstration form. The three-section staff, also known as the triple stick, was a weapon that seemed to come alive in his hands. (It seemed to come alive in my hands also, but it was mostly to my detriment, especially at the beginning when I was attempting to learn how to use it.) Such was his skill that when he wielded the spear, we thought that was the dominant weapon, and when he used the triple stick, we thought that to be the dominant weapon. He used each weapon in ways we did not think possible. Grandmaster Wong taught the form "Triple Stick versus the Spear" to me many years ago. Ever since that time, I have had great enjoyment doing this set and have performed the set in public demonstrations quite often. I cannot count the number of times I have performed this set. This is one of my favorite sets and I would like to share it with you in this book. Although I have practiced this set for a long time, I am still never totally pleased with the way that I do it. I still think I can always improve if I work just a little harder. I do not like blaming the triple stick for my own awkwardness and inability. I have performed this set with a variety of people, and trust me, each experience is different. I usually think of the set as a two-person exercise, emphasis on the "exercise" part. Others think of this set as a two-person combat form, emphasis on the "combat" part. Somewhere in between, we meet.

I have also enjoyed teaching this set to many people. For many years, I only did the triple stick part, because my teacher was always there to teach the spear part. Finally, after a few decades and upon the retirement of my teacher, I had to learn the spear part. I hope this manual allows you to practice and enjoy this set too. There are many intricacies that only a qualified instructor can show you, but if you read and study this book, it will help you understand these weapons, and possibly all other weapons, much better. Learning this set will also give you deeper insight into hand-to-hand combat and martial theory. Some insights will be revealed to you, but there are many others that you will have the pleasure of discovering on your own. As for me personally, well . . . I had to learn the hard way. Hopefully this book will make things easier for you. (I am also available to travel to teach this set, should the need and proper circumstances arise.)

Please note that this book is for cultural and educational enrichment. It is hoped that every time you refer to this book, you learn and see something new.

Be safe.

*Rick L. Wing*
August 8, 2008
San Francisco, California

# 1

# The Triple Stick: Introduction and Ancient Origins

The weapon we shall call the "triple stick" is called "sam jeet kwun" in Cantonese, or "san jie gun" in Mandarin. The literal translation of this would be "three-part stick," "three-section stick," or "three-section staff." The weapon itself is made up of three sticks connected by two sets of metal links. The wood is typically rattan or white waxwood.

One legend has it that the founder of the Northern Sung Dynasty (960–1127), Emperor Sung Tai Jo, either developed or invented this particular weapon prior to his becoming emperor. Since the emperor also is said to have created "Long Fist," it is safe to say that he had a strong martial background. One story goes that he had a favorite staff, and after this staff was somehow broken, he

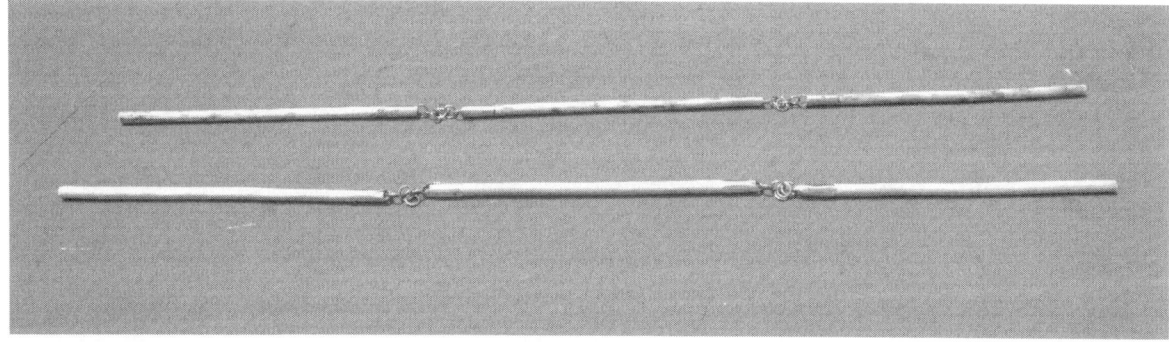

Rattan triple stick (top), white waxwood triple stick (bottom)

used a few metal links to connect the broken sticks together. After one of these sticks broke again, he connected all three parts of the sticks together with two sets of metal rings, thus creating the three-section staff. It is also possible that he may have created this weapon in one simple burst of inspiration. This is the story that is often repeated among martial artists, but I personally cannot say if it is true or not.

A number of experienced martial artists have told me that many martial origins are shrouded in myth, old legends, and secrecy, and that there are certain things that no one knows with definitive proof. Be that as it may, we shall soon show the many applications of this unique weapon known as the triple stick.

# 2
# Weapons
# and the Triple Stick

Long ago, primitive people found that they could better protect themselves against wild animals and fellow humans by fashioning weapons made from materials available to them. First they used sticks and stones, and then went on to develop spears, knives, and the like. In China, many ingenious weapons such as the hooked swords, the trident, butterfly knives, and a host of others have been developed over the centuries. Some of these are still used by martial artists today for purposes of self-defense, and more importantly in modern times, as tools for exercise and health. I myself have performed with the triple stick several times in San Francisco's nighttime Chinese New Year Parade in front of thousands, but I have also been handcuffed (by mistake) and brought down to the local police station for possession of an illegal weapon. I now prefer to practice with the triple stick as an exercise tool and a means to connect with an old cultural heritage. It is an excellent tool with which to develop coordination.

The triple stick is an extremely versatile weapon. Because of its versatility, some martial artists call the triple stick "poon lung kwun," which in Cantonese means "coiling dragon stick." This means that the triple stick should have, in the proper hands, the power, skill, speed, movement, and spirit of the dragon. It is a weapon that can be used for either short-range or long-range combat, in a small, confined space or a wide-open area. Unlike a long spear or a heavy kwandao, a triple stick can be carried easily and perhaps even concealed. It may be used in the manner of someone wielding a hard weapon, like a staff, by striking or poking someone, or it may be used in the manner of someone wielding a soft weapon, like a whip, chain, or some other type of flail, by swinging it to strike.

Although the triple stick is known to be very effective, it also takes a great deal of practice to be able to control it and use it skillfully and effectively. Mastering this weapon is much more time-consuming than mastering a staff or saber. If the triple stick is used improperly, you will be at a great disadvantage while trying to wield this weapon, and it may force you into awkward hand positions. You may lose control of it or even strike yourself by accident! This has happened to me many times. Most practitioners of the triple stick are able to tell a story of how they have injured themselves practicing. I have many of these stories also. If it is not too much of a cliché, remember, "Practice makes perfect."

In addition, by utilizing different methods of holding the triple stick, the versatility of the weapon is increased immeasurably. Carefully observe how and when the grips are changed during the set. We will show this in detail in the form described in this book.

# 3
# Four Methods
# of the Triple Stick

Various handgrips can be used with the triple stick. As each handgrip allows a different method of attack and defense, it is best to develop expertise with all of them so that you may fully exploit the capabilities of this unique weapon.

## SPLIT BEARD POSTURE

The first of these handgrips is known as "fun so kwun" in Cantonese. This may be translated as "split beard stick" and is probably the way that most people would think of holding the triple stick. As shown here, the practitioner holds the first part of the

triple stick with the left hand, and the third part of the triple stick with the right hand, with the second stick in between his hands. Holding the triple stick in this way is similar to how you might use your two arms in combat. It should be very clear how someone can use this particular handgrip to block and strike. The strength of the power of the strike is only limited by the strength and flexibility of your arms, back, and waist. Typically, a practitioner tries to close the gap on his opponent, blocking with one stick and striking with the other. The middle stick may also be used for blocking purposes.

## Split beard posture

Block                                                    Strike

Upward "X" block

High strike

Block

Strike

Low strike

Low strike

掉尾式

# SWINGING TAIL POSTURE

The second is known as "jow mei kwun," which may be translated as "swinging tail stick." The practitioner holds the first and second parts of the stick and uses the third part as a flail or "swinging tail." Great power can be generated at a short distance by using the third part of the stick as a flail.

Strike

# COILING DRAGON POSTURE

盤
龍
式

The third grip is known as "poon lung kwun," or "coiling dragon stick." The left hand may grip the first stick as before, but the right hand grips the third stick in a reverse manner. Holding the triple stick in this way allows you to use either end of the third stick to strike the opponent. Some martial artists also use "coiling dragon stick" as a generic name for the three-section staff.

## Coiling dragon posture

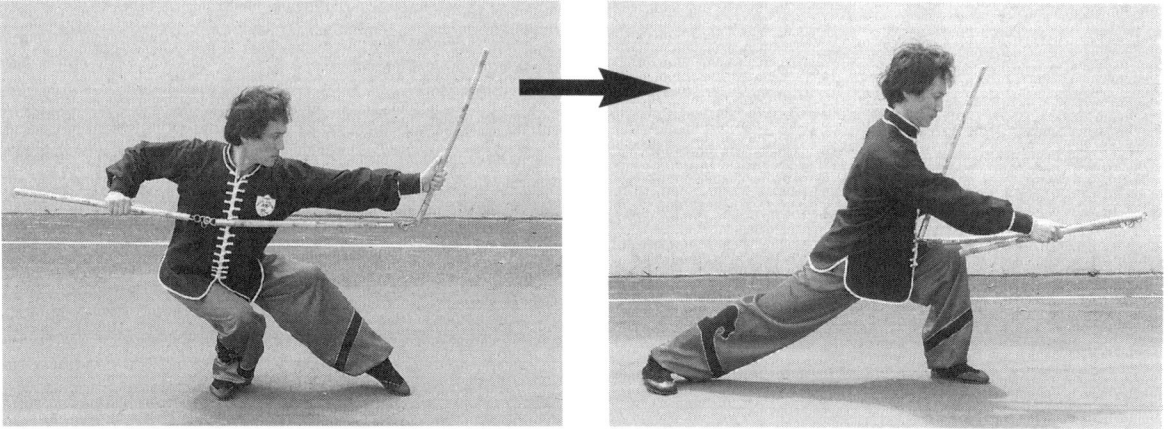

Block with left stick                    Thrust forward

# Coiling dragon posture

Downward strike

Side strike

Side strike

Block

Strike

Block

Strike

## Coiling dragon posture

Anticipate

Deflect and spin

Strike

臥龍式

# CROUCHING DRAGON POSTURE

The fourth grip is known as "ngo lung kwun," which means "crouching dragon stick." This grip uses a single hand to hold the first part, so that the third part of the stick may be used to strike the opponent at a distance. There is extreme power in using the triple stick as a long flail; and because of the quickness with which a person can change grip on the triple stick, the triple stick can change from a short weapon to a long weapon in the blink of an eye. This makes the triple stick a formidable weapon, as it has the ability to bewilder and confuse an opponent because of the unpredictability brought about by rapid grip changes.

Swing

. . . and strike

Swing from right to left

During the form that we demonstrate in this book, the grip of the person holding the triple stick changes from time to time. Be aware of this as you read the description, look at the pictures, and practice the form.

Another way that a practitioner may hold the triple stick is to use both hands to grasp the second or middle stick, and then by turning the waist and jerking both arms in the same direction, use either loose end of the triple stick as a flail to strike the opponent. Although we have some photos of this grip here, this method is not depicted in the set that we demonstrate.

Be aware that with this type of move, how the flail part rebounds off of what you strike may cause you difficulty in controlling your own weapon.

Swing

. . . and strike

# 4

# Use of the Triple Stick
# Against the Spear

The triple stick was mainly used as a weapon of personal self-defense, useful because it could be easily carried, and in practiced hands it was much more versatile than a simple long staff. Although it has been written that something similar to it was used in battlefields so that the enemy could be struck over their shields, or so that horses' legs could be caught or trapped, in general the triple stick was not considered by many to be a battlefield weapon. Spears, halberds, shields, sabers, and swords were the order of the day.

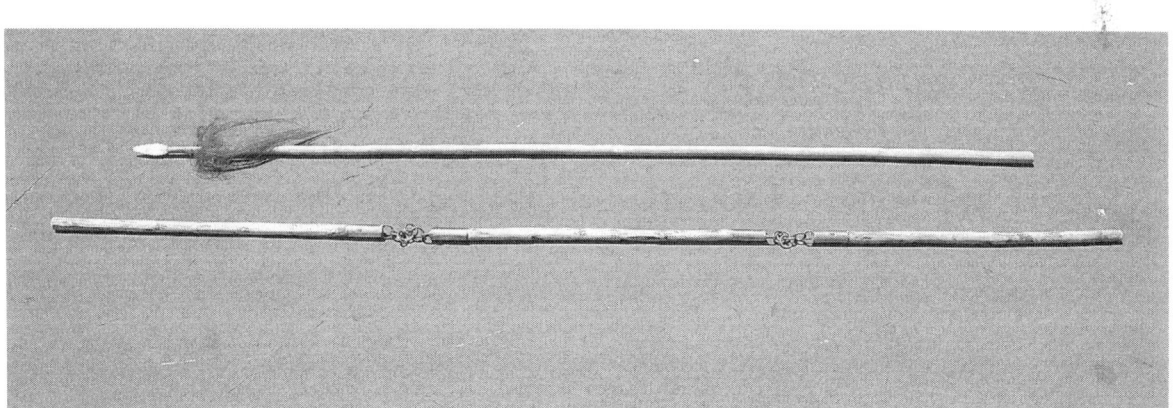

The spear and the triple stick

The spear is considered the "king of weapons" because it has the advantage of length, and it is a lethal weapon with immediate killing potential. Although of course each weapon has killing potential, it is far easier to spear an opponent in a vital spot from a distance using fairly little strength than it is to use a triple stick to strike and bludgeon him.

Because of the spear's great advantages, many martial arts systems have sparring sets, also known as "two-man sets" or "partner sets," in which a weapon is paired against the spear: saber versus spear sets, double broadsword versus spear sets, kwandao versus spear sets, double dagger versus spear sets, and a multitude of others. For hundreds of years, it has been traditional for the martial artists of China to pass down their knowledge and experience through the use of these forms. In these sparring sets, no one is supposed to "win." Each practitioner is supposed to learn the skills necessary to wield their weapon in a practical manner. In the form that we shall show, which is the Three-Section Staff versus the Spear, you will see the theory of how each weapon can be used to its own advantage and the other weapon's disadvantage. Watch carefully and see how combat is engaged at short, medium, and long range.

Note that since this is a sparring set, the moves of the three-section staff tend toward the practical. For a one-person set, using only the three-section staff, the moves may be embellished with more spinning and twirling. This is done so that the practitioner may demonstrate complete control over the weapon.

In general, the person with the spear ideally tries to maintain a long distance and attacks the triple-stick person from afar using the spear tip. However, when the person wielding the spear is up close, the spear tip may still be used to thrust at the opponent, or the butt end of the spear may be used to strike. At close range the spear tip may even be used as a dagger with which one might cut or stab one's adversary. Another strong point of the spear is that since it is a long weapon, the practitioner, using both hands on the weapon, may easily exert leverage and strength at both short and long range.

The practitioner who wields the triple stick needs to be able to exploit the weapon's versatility and uniqueness. To do this requires a great deal of skill, dexterity, and ingenuity. To fully exploit the triple stick's capabilities, one needs to practice with it and train with it diligently. The triple stick is said to be the weapon of choice among advanced practitioners of the martial arts. (Personally, given the choice, I think most of us would rather take the spear.)

## The long reach of the spear

The spear thrusts high and is blocked

The spear thrusts low to the knee

## The spear jabs to create the opening, and then thrusts elsewhere

Spear draws back

Spear feints upward

Withdraws

. . . and thrusts

## The spear used as a staff

Strike from above

## The spear disarming the triple stick by hooking the weapon away

Hook

. . . and pull

Mid-level attack: using the butt end of the spear
as a close-range weapon

High-level attack: using the butt end of the spear
as a close-range weapon

# The triple stick at close quarters

Block

Strike to chest using the joint

Block

Strike to groin using the tip

# 5
# History of the Form

A great deal of instruction in the martial arts took place at the Jing Mo Athletic Association in Shanghai in the 1920s.

The famed Jing Mo Athletic Association ("Jing Wu" in Mandarin) attempted to revive the spirit of the Chinese people by using the martial arts as a vehicle to promote health, exercise, and the propagation of Chinese culture. They actively sought out the best instructors for their students.

Among the many instructors, four should be noted here: Lo Kwan Yuk, who taught "Seven Star Praying Mantis"; Chan Tzi Cheng, who taught "Eagle Claw"; Lo Wai Chang, who taught northern style; and Chiu Lin Wo, who also taught northern style.

One of Chiu Lin Wo's instructors was the renowned Fok Yuen Gap ("Ho Yuan Chia" in Mandarin). Fok Yuen Gap, who taught the My Jong style, is credited as the founder of the Jing Mo Athletic Association in 1909, although he passed away only a few months after its founding. Of the many things taught by Chiu Lin Wo, he is most associated with the twelve rows of Tam Tuei. Tam Tuei, which literally translates as "Tam's leg" or "Tam's kick," is an extremely famous and foundational northern form. Yip Yee Ting, a well-known instructor of My Jong Law Hon in Hong Kong, also learned from Chiu Lin Wo.

Chiu Lin Wo taught the form "Triple Stick versus the Spear" to Poon Mao Yung, another master of northern style. Poon Mao Yung, also a master of a style called "Five Direction Fist," wrote the

羅　光　玉

Lo Kwan Yuk

陳　子　正

Chan Tzi Cheng

昌 煒 盧

Lo Wai Chang

和 連 趙

Chiu Lin Wo

Fok Yuen Gap

book "Sam Jeet Kwun To Sut," which means "A Guide to the Three-Section Staff with Photos and Explanation," published by the Wah Lun Company in Taiwan. The Chinese writing used in this book was of a very old style, and not all people with facility in the Chinese language could easily read this manual.

Instead of demonstrating the usefulness of the triple stick by showing many applications against various weapons, we choose to demonstrate the intricacies of the triple stick against the spear, since the spear is such a formidable weapon in its own right. Applications of the triple stick against other weapons may then be inferred, and this form should suggest a myriad of applications. Any particular technique or segment of this form can be taken out and practiced over and over again if so desired.

The benefits of learning this form are many. Simply by doing this form with a partner, a person develops aerobic capacity, improved musculature, and increased coordination skills. Aside from the health and exercise aspects, the practitioner also learns concepts of offense and defense using two old-style weapons, the spear and the triple stick. Practicing this form also enables you to relive the days of old China and lets you see how people utilized weapons in an era long past.

I learned this form from my esteemed instructor, Wong Jack Man, Sifu, founder of the Jing Mo Athletic Association of San Francisco.

Wong Jack Man

# 6

# The Form: Triple Stick versus the Spear

When practicing this form with a partner, please be very careful so as not to cause injury. This is a set for advanced and experienced practitioners only and should be treated as such. Use control at all times. Control, control, control! For the person using the spear (**S**), be careful not to thrust directly at the person holding the triple stick (**TS**). Instead, aim the tip of the spear slightly away from the vital area so that if **TS** misses the block, there will be no injury. If **S** does thrust directly at **TS**, **S** should always maintain the capability to withdraw the spear tip should **TS** fail to block in time. We also recommend using a tapered stick instead of a spear for practice. This is much safer.

Consider these notes to be approximate instructions, as both practitioners have to constantly and immediately adjust their stances and body positioning to adapt to their partner's movements. Note also that although people can learn a movement in the set, they may give the same movement a completely different flavor when applying the move. For instance, **S** has the option of using long, deep thrusts against **TS**, or he may just use light, quick jabs. In opposition, **TS** may block using hard strikes against the spear, or he may simply use light deflections and parries to remain in slight contact with the spear. There may be cases made for both approaches, and the advantages and disadvantages of each should always be examined. This is what my teacher carefully explained to me.

For each of the practitioners, always be aware of where you are striking and where you are being struck. Be careful not to strike your partner on the hands when you get up close. For the person wielding the spear, be mindful of where the tip is at all times. Always be aware of distance when thrusting the spear. The person with the triple stick can usually exert more control over the weapon, as it is usually close to the body. The timing between the partners must be exact, especially when the triple stick is used as a flail since the triple stick cannot easily be pulled back once it is set in motion.

Because the spear is a very dominating weapon, there are about forty-eight offensive moves of the spear and twenty defensive moves, while the triple stick has about thirty-three offensive moves and thirty-nine defensive moves. I only counted moves of the weapon itself and did not count evasive moves of the body. Some of the moves could be very subtle in their characterization.

Some sections of this chapter include "reverse views," photos taken from the opposite side in order to better show what is happening in the movement. Not all of these photos are exact replicas of their "front view" counterparts, but most of them are close. Where a reverse-view photo does not match up with any of the other front-view photos, we have included a short explanation of where it falls in the sequence of movements (e.g. after figure 2, but before figure 3).

This is a set that can be examined again and again so that you may see the dynamic interplay between these two classical and significant weapons. This set may also be dissected so that a practitioner may see how these concepts relate to hand-to-hand self-defense. Hopefully, the practitioner will come to a higher level of understanding of personal defense, whether it be armed or unarmed. The intelligent construction of this form should be studied and analyzed very carefully. Of course, once you have mastered the form and the moves flow naturally from within you, you are then well on your way to thinking up new and better applications. In other words, once you have mastered the form, you can then go beyond the form. This is the way to think about sets in the Chinese martial arts.

The best way to learn this form, as with most other forms, is in small increments. It is probably best to learn the movements in groups of three to five at a time. Learning in small increments will give you time to do the movements properly, and will allow you to perfect the movements and retain them better. When you learn a set very quickly, the rate at which you learn it is typically the same rate at which you forget it. Do not be in a hurry to rush through and complete the form as fast as you can. If you go slowly through the form while you are learning it, you will better be able to see the intricacies and subtleties of each weapon. As many people know, the martial arts are not just for learning physical skills but also mental skills. Patience in learning will reap rewards. Take your time with this form and savor the movements, a few at a time.

One last cautionary note: This set is *not* a competition as to who can be more careless. If you perceive that your partner is not going to do a particular block or parry in time, do not follow through with your strike and hit your partner! Be aware of what is happening at all times, and have the common sense and responsibility to pull your weapon back so no one gets injured. If you injure your partner, you are at fault for not having proper control over your weapon. Be extremely careful when practicing this set!

**TS** designates the person wielding the triple stick.
**S** designates the person using the spear.

# 1: STAND AT ATTENTION.

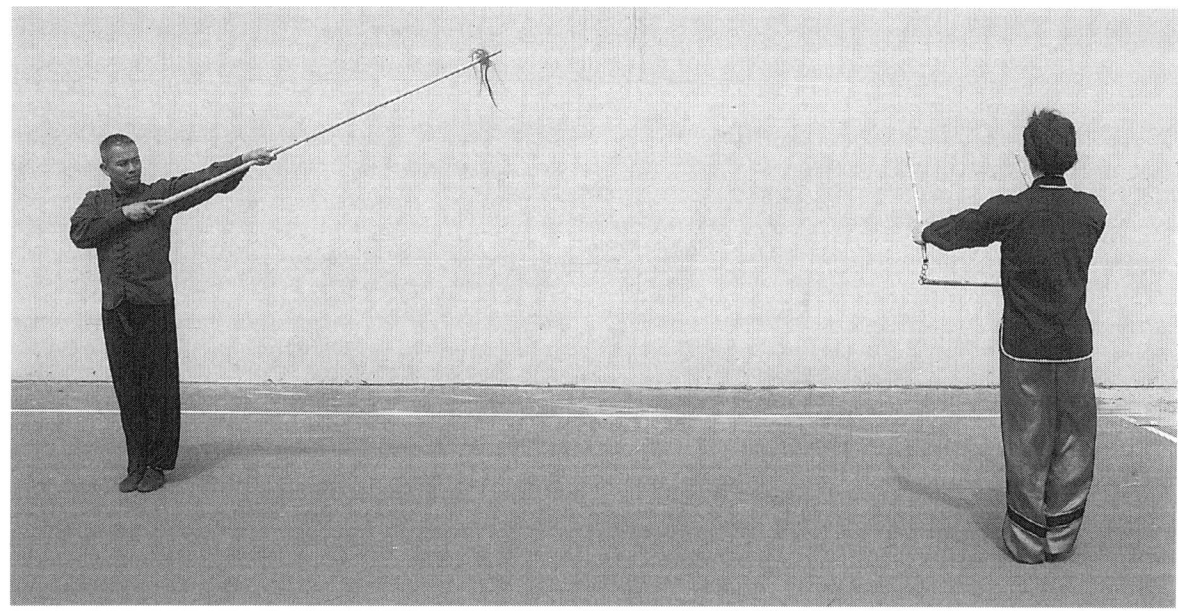

Front view

The person with the spear (**S**) stands with the spear pointing up and to the left at a forty-five-degree angle.

The person with the triple stick (**TS**) holds the left stick in his left hand and the right stick in his right hand, with the middle part hanging near his abdomen. This particular grip is called the "split beard" grip.

Reverse view

# 2: OPENING POSITION.

**5**

S takes a step out and to the right with his right leg. He lifts the back part of the spear up with his right hand. When he brings his right hand back down, he steps into a left cat stance and the spear tip points up. He is now in the "ready" position.

TS initially pushes both sticks downward and stamps his right foot. He revolves the sticks in a complete circle, steps into a left cat stance, and crosses the right stick over the left. TS is now in the "ready" position.

Reverse view of 5

## 3: **S** THRUSTS THE SPEAR AT **TS**'S HEAD.

Depending on the exact distance, **S** may shuffle forward—left foot, stamp right foot, left foot—and then thrust the spear at **TS**'s head. **S** is using the advantage of the length of the spear by attacking **TS** from a distance. This is the spear at its most deadly.

**TS** uses a brushing motion from left to right and blocks the spear from the inside.

Note: As a hidden application, **TS** may use his right stick to block the spear thrust, and use his left stick to strike at **S**'s left hand. Although this is possible, typically **S** thrusts the spear out and withdraws it so fast that **TS** does not have a chance to do this.

Reverse view of 4

# 4: S THRUSTS THE SPEAR AT TS'S MIDSECTION.

S withdraws the spear and shoots it out again at **TS**'s midsection.

**TS** lifts up the left stick and brings the right part of the stick downward so that the middle section of the triple stick deflects the spear tip to the left side. TS stays in the left cat stance.

Reverse view of 3

## 5: **S** THRUSTS THE SPEAR AT **TS**'S LEFT SHIN.

S withdraws the spear and shoots it at **TS**'s left shin. Some using the spear would shoot it at **TS**'s knee area. Either is acceptable.

Note that in the first series of movements of the form, **S** immediately put **TS** on the defensive. It is from this vantage that the spear is most deadly and possesses the greatest advantage.

**TS** lifts up his left leg so as not to be struck by the spear tip. At the same time, he blocks down and to the left with the left stick.

Reverse view (comes after figure 2 but before figure 3)

Reverse view of 4

## 6: **TS** COUNTERATTACKS AND STRIKES AT **S**'S HEAD.

Reverse view of 1

Reverse view of 3

Now it is **TS**'s turn to go on the offensive after having parried three consecutive thrusts of the spear. **TS** steps down with his left foot and forward with his right leg. **TS** attempts to hit the side of **S**'s head with the right stick. **TS** ends in a right horse stance.

S withdraws into a left cat stance and pulls the spear back with force so that the upper part of the spear blocks **TS**'s strike. This is a strong block by **S**!

Reverse view of 4

# 7: **TS** FOLLOWS UP WITH AN ATTACK TO **S**'S MIDSECTION.

**4**

Since **TS** has now closed the gap with **S**, **TS** steps in with his left foot moving behind his right leg, and assumes a right T-stance. He attempts to hit **S** with the inner part, or joint, of the right stick. One might say that **TS** is attempting to flow into **S**'s openings.

**S** withdraws his left foot to assume a right cat stance and uses the bottom part of the spear to deflect the triple stick to the left side. Stances and hand positions vary from practitioner to practitioner as necessary. **S** may use the middle part of the spear to block, may assume a horse stance, or may assume a right horse stance. All are acceptable. Both practitioners may vary things slightly so long as it does not interrupt the flow and continuity of the form. As in actual combat, stances will constantly need to be adjusted because of the many variables involved.

Reverse view of 4

## 8: **S** ATTACKS BY STRIKING DOWNWARD AT **TS**'S HEAD.

S shifts his right foot forward into a right horse stance. Simultaneously, he uses his left hand to push the spear down toward TS's head. His right hand also helps pull the spear downward, and his right hand ends near his right hip. S is now using the spear as a cudgel. S has the potential to generate a great deal of force with a strike such as this.

TS defends by lifting the right stick to meet the spear strike. He withdraws his left leg so that 60 percent of his weight is on his left leg and 40 percent of his weight is on his right leg. Both the left stick and the right stick end up pointing in the same direction (to the left side). TS should push upward with strength and brace himself against a hard strike from the shaft of the spear.

Reverse view of 3

# 9: **TS** ATTACKS **S**'S HEAD.

**3**

**TS** swings the right stick in a downward clockwise circle toward **S**'s head. He shifts into a right horse stance and attempts to regain the advantage with a quick turn of his right stick.

**S** moves both of his hands to the left and plants the butt end of the spear on the ground for added stability. He uses the center part of the spear to block the strike of the triple stick. His left hand is on the top, his right hand is below, and he assumes a strong square horse stance. He may slide his left hand up and his right hand down so as to not get struck on his fingers.

Reverse view of 3

# 10: S USES THE BUTT END OF THE SPEAR TO ATTACK **TS**'S HEAD.

Reverse view of 2

Reverse view of 3

**5**

**S** uses his right hand to guide the back end of the spear to strike at **TS**'s head. The back end of the spear moves clockwise from left to right. **S** shifts back into a left-leaning horse stance. He may slide his right hand closer to his left hand, leaning back, to move himself out of danger while at the same time threatening **TS**. He then reverses the direction of the spear to strike from right to left and slightly upward.

**TS** shifts into a left horse stance and leans backward, letting the butt end of the spear go over his right shoulder. To prevent **S** from using the spear to strike his face on the return stroke, **TS** revolves his right stick in an almost complete counterclockwise motion, and then finally checks the upward motion of the spear to make sure that the spear does not come back up and toward **TS**'s face.

Reverse view of 5

# 11: **S** THRUSTS THE SPEAR AT THE BACK OF **TS**'S RIGHT LEG.

5

S lifts up his right leg, pushes off with his left leg, and switches into a left horse stance. Alternatively, **S** could step back and stamp the ground with his right foot and then switch quickly into a left horse stance. Simultaneously, he pulls his right hand to the end of the spear, uses his left hand to aim the spear, and thrusts the spear tip forward toward the back of **TS**'s right leg.

To avoid the spear thrust toward his right leg, **TS** steps his right leg past the front of his left leg into a right T-stance. He then uses his right stick to deflect the spear tip by using a right-to-left blocking motion.

Reverse view of 5

# 12: **S** ATTEMPTS TO SPEAR **TS**'S BACK.

Depending on how far **TS** steps, **S** shuffles up, withdraws the spear, and then thrusts the spear at **TS**'s back.

**TS** quickly turns to his left into a left cat stance and uses the left stick to deflect the spear tip at his left side. **TS** should turn very quickly so that **S** does not have the chance to spear him in the back.

Reverse view of 5

# 13: S ATTEMPTS TO SPEAR TS'S CHEST.

Again, depending on the distance, **S** shuffles forward, pulls the spear back, and then shoots it out at **TS**'s chest.

**TS** takes a step back with his left foot and moves into a right cat stance. He uses the right stick to block the spear tip by moving the right stick from right to left.

Reverse view of 4

# 14: **S** THRUSTS THE SPEAR AT **TS**'S HEAD.

Reverse view of 1

Reverse view of 2

**4**

S again shuffles up and tries to spear **TS**'s head. As you can see, one of the great advantages of the spear is that **S** can constantly put **TS** on the defensive by maintaining distance and by thrusting with the spear.

    **TS**, in an attempt to regain the offensive, shifts into a right horse stance and uses an "X" block (right stick on the inside) to deflect the spear tip upward. With this particular spear attack, since the dangerous part of the spear is the tip, all **TS** needs to do is to make sure that the spear tip goes past the sticks and above his head.

Reverse view of 4

## 15: **TS** STRIKES AT **S**'S LEFT KNEE.

**TS** is now on the offensive after being on the defensive for the past few moves. One way for **TS** to gain an advantage is to quickly move in closer to **S**. **TS** slides his left (rear) leg forward, and then his right leg forward, to close the gap between him and **S**. He attempts to strike **S**'s left knee or shin with the right stick.

In defense, **S** maintains downward pressure against the triple stick and lifts his left leg out of the way so as not to be struck by the right stick of **TS**.

Reverse view of 4

## 16: TS STRIKES AT S'S RIGHT KNEE.

Reverse view of 1

Reverse view of 2

Maintaining the "X" block, **TS** slides his left leg forward all the way past his right leg so that he is in a horse stance with his left foot forward. At the same time, he attempts to strike **S**'s right knee with his left stick.

As **TS** is rushing in, **S** maintains downward pressure on **TS** by pushing down with the spear. He brings his left leg all the way back, withdraws his spear, and then, while shifting into a right cat stance, pushes down with his left hand to use the lower part of the spear to protect his right leg. Here, **S** is using the lower part of the spear as a defensive wall.

Reverse view of 3

Reverse view of 5

# 17: **S** ATTACKS **TS**'S HEAD.

S takes a small clockwise step to the left with his right foot, followed by a forward step with his left foot. S now uses the top part of the spear in a clockwise downward motion to strike at TS's head. S ends up in a high left horse stance.

TS deflects this by following the motion of the spear. He uses the left stick in a counterclockwise motion upward to protect his face. TS is in a left cat stance.

Reverse view of 4

# 18:  S ATTEMPTS TO CUT TS'S LEFT LOWER LEG.

Because **TS** has parried his strike, **S** continues his clockwise downward motion and drops into a low left horse stance while attempting to cut the lower part of **TS**'s left leg by moving the spear tip from right to left.

To avoid this, **TS** puts his weight on his right leg and lifts up his left leg.

The reverse-view photo shows **S** just before he sweeps down with the spear and attacks **TS**'s left leg.

Reverse view of 1

## 19: **TS** GOES BACK ON THE OFFENSIVE BY ATTEMPTING TO STRIKE **S**'S HEAD.

**3**

To avoid the cutting motion of **S**, **TS** lifted up his left leg. Now, **TS** pushes off with his right leg, switches stance, and falls into a right horse stance. At the same time, he attacks **S**'s head by using his right stick in a downward strike.

S blocks this by pushing both hands straight up, and uses the body of the spear to protect his head. He steps back into a right horse stance.

Reverse view (comes after figure 2 but before figure 3)

Reverse view of 3

# 20: S ATTEMPTS TO HIT **TS**'S HEAD FROM THE LEFT (DOWN) AND THEN THE RIGHT (UP).

Reverse view of 2

Reverse view of 3

S presses down with the spear in a clockwise motion to strike at **TS**'s head.

**TS** bends his head slightly back and to the left to avoid being struck. He moves the right part of the triple stick in a complete counterclockwise motion to stay ahead of the spear.

**S** brings the spear back up in a counterclockwise motion to strike at **TS**'s head. **TS** moves his right stick down to complete the counterclockwise circle. He uses the right stick to make sure the ascending spear does not hit him in the face.

Reverse view of 4

## 21: S ATTEMPTS TO SPEAR THE RIGHT SIDE OF TS'S BODY.

Reverse view of 1

Reverse view of 2

S slides forward and thrusts the spear at **TS**'s body. He is in a left horse stance momentarily, then his right foot slides up.

**TS** avoids this blow by taking a step back with his right foot and dropping into a right horse stance. He uses the middle section of the triple stick to deflect the spear tip by using a left-to-right backward motion.

Reverse view of 4

## 22: S ADVANCES USING THE BUTT END OF THE SPEAR TO STRIKE AT TS'S HEAD.

S slides his right leg forward and twists his body counterclockwise so that he may strike at **TS**'s head using the butt end of the spear in a forward motion.

**TS**, using the power generated by taking a step back with his left foot, turning the body counterclockwise, and using a right-to-left motion with the right stick, blocks this, using force against force.

Reverse view of 1

Reverse view of 3

## 23: S ADVANCES FORWARD AND ATTACKS AGAIN WITH THE BODY OF THE SPEAR.

S twists his body clockwise to strike at **TS**'s head.

**TS** counters this by twisting his body clockwise, settling into a right T-stance, and using the left stick to block the spear by striking the spear in a left-to-right motion. Even though **TS** is on the defensive, he is still attempting to close the gap in anticipation of his own retaking of the offensive.

Reverse view of 3

## 24: **TS** ATTEMPTS TO STRIKE **S**'S HEAD.

**TS** uses his left stick to push the spear to the side. He steps forward with his left leg into a left horse stance. He attempts to strike the top of **S**'s head with the right stick.

**S** drops his left leg back to assume a right horse stance. (Alternatively, some using the spear do not change stance but stay in a left horse stance since the attack from **TS** may come too quickly. Either is acceptable.) **S** pushes the spear upward to block the strike with the middle of the spear.

Reverse view of 2

Reverse view of 3

## 25: S ATTEMPTS TO COME OVER THE TOP AND STRIKE **TS**'S HEAD.

After receiving the strike of **TS**, **S** counterattacks by drawing the spear back with his right hand and pushing down with his left hand. **S** may step forward into a left horse stance or may step in place by withdrawing his right leg first and then stepping up with his left leg to end in a left horse stance. Either is acceptable, as these adjustments are constantly necessary when doing a two-person form.

**TS** stays in the left horse stance. He quickly lets go of the right stick with his right hand, and the right stick falls to his left side.

Reverse view of 3

He repositions his right hand on the middle stick. His right hand moves to his left side and above his left shoulder. He uses the middle section to protect his head. **TS** exerts some force upward just in case the strike from the spear is particularly hard. **TS** has now changed to using the "swinging tail" grip for defensive purposes.

## Alternate Views of 3

**Grip A**

Reverse view of Grip A

Reverse view of Grip B

Some people wielding the triple stick prefer to use the middle part of the stick and let the spear fall between their hands (Grip A). This particular grip allows for more stability. Others prefer a grip where the spear strike falls to the left of both of their hands (Grip B). This lessens the chances of their hands being struck by the spear, though the grip weakens the strength and stability of the block.

## 26: **TS** ATTACKS **S**'S LEGS.

**TS** revolves his hands clockwise to push the spear to his left side using either his left forearm or his left stick to push or strike the spear. **TS** pushes off with his right (rear) foot, and switches to a horse stance with his right leg forward. He uses the right section of the triple stick as a flail with which to strike **S**'s legs. **TS** has now switched to using the "swinging tail" grip for offensive purposes. This is a very tricky and subtle move of the triple stick and one that is usually very unexpected by the opponent.

S pushes off with his right leg and leaps up to let the flail part pass under his legs.

Reverse view of 3

Reverse view of 4

# 27: **S** ATTEMPTS TO SPEAR **TS**'S CHEST.

Immediately upon landing, left leg then right leg coming down to the ground, **S** attempts to spear **TS** in the chest.

**TS** steps forward and to the left to avoid the spear tip. He throws the flail part over the spear in a short clockwise motion with his right hand to attempt to hook the front part of the spear downward.

Reverse view of 4

## 28: **TS** STRIKES AT **S**'S HEAD.

Because **TS** has temporarily trapped the spear, **TS** attempts to keep the front end of the spear immobilized and pointed downward so as not to cause harm. **TS** steps forward with his left leg and attempts to strike **S**'s head with the left stick.

**S** pulls the spear down and back to get out of the control of the triple stick. He uses the body of the spear to block the incoming strike. He slides his left foot back and retreats into a left cat stance, with his weight on his right leg.

Reverse view of 5

## 29: **S** PUSHES FORWARD AND ATTEMPTS TO SWEEP **TS**'S LEGS.

While **TS** is pushing forward with the left stick, **S** withdraws the spear a few inches and drops more of his weight back onto his right leg to gain some momentum with which to push forward. He then pushes forward with the body of the spear. As his weight is transferred to his left leg, **S** pushes off with his left leg and jumps forward with his right leg. He lands on his right leg and steps down and forward with his left leg. His right leg steps forward and down into a right T-stance. At the same time he rotates the spear in a circular, clockwise motion and his left hand guides the sweeping motion with the spear as he attempts to sweep **TS**'s legs or strike him across the shins.

Reverse view of 3

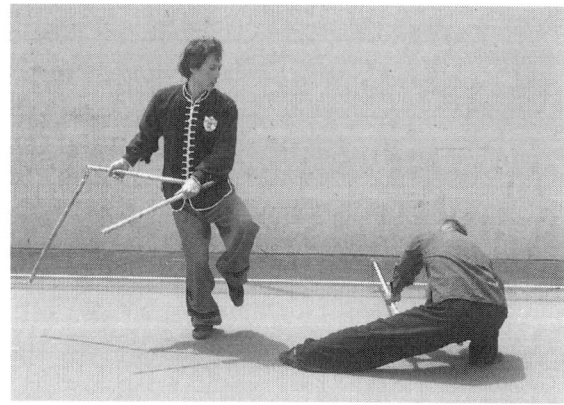

Reverse view of 7

# 30: **TS** AVOIDS THE SWEEP. **S** TURNS AND ATTEMPTS TO SPEAR **TS** IN THE FACE.

To avoid the sweep, **TS** rears back on his right (rear) leg and, pushing off with his right leg, jumps over the oncoming spear. He also guides the flail part of the triple stick with an overhand swinging motion of his right hand. (If **S** is slow in dropping down to sweep **TS**'s legs, **TS** has the option of striking **S** in the head using the flail part of the triple stick. As another application, **TS** could also strike straight down at **S**'s head using the flail when **S** is executing his sweep with the spear. Although this motion is not depicted, the practitioner should understand that it is implied in the form.) When **TS** comes down to the ground, he quickly and immediately turns to his left so that his own back is not exposed and to see what **S** is doing.

After **S** fails in his attempt to sweep **TS**, he turns to his left and immediately shoots out the spear in an attempt to regain the advantage. **S** is in a left horse stance.

**TS** sees the spear thrust coming and uses his left stick to parry the spear in a quick right-to-left motion.

Reverse view of 2

Reverse view of 6

## 31:   **TS** USES THE FLAIL END OF THE TRIPLE STICK TO STRIKE AT THE LEFT SIDE OF **S**'S BODY.

After blocking, **TS** immediately shifts into a left horse stance and uses the flail end of the triple stick to strike at the left side of **S**'s body. The right arm and the turning of the waist supply the power behind the strike.

**S** sees the strike coming and quickly withdraws the spear in a downward circular, clockwise motion to block the strike.

Reverse view of 3

# 32: **S** STRIKES BACK AT **TS**'S CHEST USING A DOWNWARD MOTION.

S continues the big clockwise circle with his spear and comes right back at **TS**'s head in a downward strike. This is a very powerful blow of the spear.

**TS** drops his left leg back and assumes a right horse stance. He uses his left leg and shoulders to brace against the spear strike because of the great momentum gathered by the spear in movement 31. Be prepared to be on the receiving end of a hard strike. **TS**'s right leg is at a forty-five-degree angle to his left leg.

Reverse view of 4

# 33: TS STRIKES AT S'S HEAD.

After **TS** blocks the powerful blow of **S**, **TS** pushes his left stick down and to the right to force the spear out of the way. He then uses his right hand (placed on the middle stick) to guide the flail to strike directly down at the top of **S**'s head.

**S** blocks straight up with the body of the spear. **S** withdraws his left leg and shifts into a right horse stance for stability.

Reverse view of 2

Reverse view of 4

# 34: S STRIKES BACK AT TS'S HEAD.

The flail end of the triple stick swings to the left side of **TS**'s body. As seen from the perspective of **S**, the flail end of the triple stick goes off to the right side of **S**.

S may withdraw his right leg slightly to gather power to push off from his right leg. He then steps forward with his left leg and shifts into a left horse stance as he strikes down at the top of **TS**'s head. As before, to get force into the blow, he slides his right hand down the spear and pulls with his right hand, while at the same

5

time sliding his left hand up the spear so that he may press down even harder with the spear.

**TS** shifts his right hand over to and above his own left shoulder and raises his left hand slightly. This allows the middle section of the triple stick to be used to block the downward strike of the spear. **TS** assumes a left horse stance, braced for a hard hit from the spear.

Reverse view of 5

# 35: **TS** ATTEMPTS TO WHIP **S**'S LEGS.

**4**

TS rotates both arms in a clockwise level circle. His left arm or the left stick pushes the spear out to the left side. **TS** pushes off with his right leg and switches stance so that his right leg is forward. **TS** attempts to whip **S**'s legs with the flail part of the triple stick by swinging his right arm from the right side to the left side in a circular motion. **TS** ends up in a horse stance with his right leg forward.

To avoid this blow, **S** lifts up his left leg to remove it from danger. He pushes off with his right leg and jumps up and over the flail end of the triple stick.

Reverse view of 3

Reverse view of 4

## 36: **S** THRUSTS THE SPEAR AT **TS**'S CHEST.

**4**

Upon landing, left foot first, right foot second, **S** immediately shoots out the spear toward **TS**'s chest.

   **TS** withdraws his right leg into a right cat stance and hooks the front part of the spear by swinging the flail end up and over the spear using a slight left-to-right clockwise motion.

Reverse view of 4

# 37: **TS** ATTEMPTS TO STRIKE **S** IN THE HEAD.

TS exerts downward pressure on the spear with his right hand. While stepping forward with his left leg into a left horse stance, he attempts to strike S in the face or head with the left part of the triple stick.

S withdraws into a left cat stance and brings his left hand back and up to guide the spear so that the middle part of the spear gives him protection.

Reverse view of 4

# 38: USING THE FLAIL END OF THE TRIPLE STICK, **TS** ATTACKS **S**'S LEGS.

**TS** rears back on his right leg and then quickly switches stance into a horse stance with his right leg forward. He swings the flail end of the triple stick from right to left at **S**'s legs.

S pushes off with his right leg and jumps up and over the flail end of the triple stick so as not to be injured by the strike of the flail. At the same time, S holds his left hand near the spear tip end, slides his right hand up toward the spear tip, and attempts to use the butt end of the spear in a swinging motion to strike at TS's head.

To someone observing this part of the sparring set, it will seem as if the actions of TS and S are simultaneous; however, in actual combat, the person who strikes first will clearly have the advantage.

Reverse view (comes after figure 1 but before figure 2)

Reverse view of 3

## 39: S ATTEMPTS TO SWEEP THE BACK OF **TS**'S RIGHT LEG WITH THE LOWER PART OF THE SPEAR.

Upon landing, **S** uses his right hand to pull back on the spear so that it sweeps toward the back of **TS**'s right leg.

**TS** sees this sweep coming and lifts up his right leg. Pushing off with his left leg, he jumps up and rotates his body in a clockwise direction, while swinging the flail end of the triple stick from the left side to the right side in an attempt to strike **S**.

Reverse view of 4

## 40: S ATTEMPTS TO STRIKE TS'S HEAD.

After using the back end of the spear to attempt to sweep **TS**, **S** rises up on his right leg and lifts his left leg up. He attempts to strike **TS** in the head with his spear. **S** slides his right hand down the spear and his left hand up the spear to get more power into the movement.

However, **TS** notices this and uses the left part of the triple stick to block this strike. **TS** moves the left part of the triple stick from left to right to accomplish this block. **TS** stands on his right leg with his left leg off the ground.

Reverse view of 3

## 41: **TS** ATTEMPTS TO STRIKE **S**'S HEAD.

**TS** forces the spear to the right side with the left stick and steps down with his left foot, dropping down into a left horse stance. While coming down into the left horse stance, he guides the flail end of the triple stick down on top of **S**'s head using his right hand on the middle stick.

**S** brings his left foot back and assumes a right horse stance. He raises the spear upward to protect his head and blocks straight up with the body of the spear.

Reverse view of 4

## 42: **TS** CATCHES THE FLAIL PART OF THE TRIPLE STICK OUT OF THE AIR.

**S** exerts so much upward force with the body of the spear that the flail part of the triple stick is bounced straight back. If **S** has good fortune, the flail part of the triple stick might bounce back and strike **TS** on the head; however, this is not to be the case.

**TS** uses his right hand to quickly catch the flail part of his triple stick.

Note: Moves such as these are meant to teach dexterity and are unlikely to be used in actual combat. This movement has a certain "performance" aspect about it.

Reverse view of 2

## 43: S STRIKES DOWNWARD AT TS'S HEAD.

After **S** blocks the flail part of the triple stick, he immediately uses his spear to strike at **TS**'s head by sliding his right hand down the spear and back and sliding his left hand forward and down along the body of the spear. **S** switches stance by stepping up with his left leg into a left horse stance.

After **TS** catches the flail part of the triple stick in his right hand, he assumes a left cat stance and uses the right stick, held at a forty-five-degree angle above horizontal, to absorb the blow of the spear. Stretching the triple stick a bit to improve the stability of the block makes it easier to absorb the blow. Holding the triple stick with this particular grip is known as the "coiling dragon stick."

Reverse view of 3

## 44: **TS** CLEARS THE SPEAR OUT OF THE WAY.

TS uses the left stick, in a quick right-to-left motion, to knock the spear to the left. This gives **TS** the time he needs to attempt his next move.

**S** feels his spear knocked to the right side and momentarily loses control of his weapon.

Reverse view of 2

# 45: THE CROUCHING DRAGON IS UNLEASHED!

After **TS** knocks the spear to the side with his left stick, he continues with this motion and releases the left stick. Using his right hand only, **TS** attempts to whip **S**'s legs using the triple stick as a long flail. **TS** gathers power and momentum for the blow by pushing off with his right leg and jumping up, switching stance so that his right leg is now forward. **TS** gets power into this movement by using his entire body. Holding the triple stick with one hand like this is known as the "crouching dragon stick." The short weapon has instantly become a long weapon!

S leaps up to avoid being struck in the legs by the triple stick. **S** may jump up high (depending on the height of the attack), with both legs simultaneously, and land with both legs at the same time. As **S** leaps up, he uses his right hand to guide the spear back into the control of his left hand. (Alternatively, **S** may leap up high by pushing off with his right foot and then land left foot first, followed by his right foot. Either way of jumping is acceptable.)

Reverse view of 4

# 46: S RESUMES THE ATTACK BY ATTEMPTING TO SPEAR TS'S CHEST OR HEAD.

TS catches the end of the triple stick in his left hand. Knowing that S is intent on spearing him, and needing to buy some time since he has missed his opportunity, he takes a big step back with his right foot.

Once S regains control of his spear and lands, he immediately shuffles forward and attempts to spear TS in the chest or head.

Once TS has the left stick firmly in hand, he is able to parry the spear with a strong left-to-right side motion. His hand position is now in the "coiling dragon" grip. In anticipation of the next move, TS pulls the right stick back with his right hand.

Reverse view of 2

Reverse view of 7

# 47: THE COILING DRAGON STRIKES FROM BELOW.

**6**

To even the odds, **TS** must again attempt to get close to overcome the advantage of the spear. **TS** charges forward, first with his right foot and then his left foot. At the same time that he is stepping forward, he is winding up and getting ready to push the joint part between the middle stick and the right stick into **S**'s abdomen.

When **TS** gets close to **S**, he pulls the left stick back toward himself and thrusts the right stick forward so as to dig into **S**. **TS** shifts into a left horse stance.

**S** steps back with his left foot into a horse stance and uses the middle part of the spear to parry the joint part of the triple stick to the left and outside.

Reverse view of 6

## 48: THE COILING DRAGON STRIKES FROM ABOVE.

**TS** steps his right foot behind his left leg and spins his body clockwise. He is attempting to come around to the unprotected side of **S** and strike him in the side of the head with the tip of the triple stick. (As a variation, **TS** could use the point to attack upward from down below, to attack **S**'s lower ribs. Remember, it is important to discuss any changes in the set with your partner first. No surprises, please.)

**5**

S turns his body slightly to the right, shifts his weight onto his right foot, and assumes a right cat stance while he raises the butt end of the spear. He uses the lower part of the spear to deflect the strike of the point of the triple stick.

Reverse view of 1

Reverse view of 5

# 49: THE SPEAR STRIKES FROM ABOVE.

S follows his own momentum and moves his right leg back to assume a left horse stance. This helps provide power as he strikes downward with the spear onto the top of **TS**'s head.

TS raises the right part of the triple stick to block the spear. The part of the triple stick used to block is between the joint and the right hand. As in all other moves, be careful that you do not allow the spear to strike your right hand.

Reverse view of 2

Reverse view of 3

# 50: THE COILING DRAGON STRIKES STRAIGHT AHEAD.

TS uses the left point of the triple stick to strike straight out at S's chest. TS is in a right horse stance.

S withdraws his left leg slightly and assumes a left cat stance. He raises the lower part of the spear to use the body of the spear for deflection purposes. S parries the point of the triple stick slightly to the right.

Reverse view of 2

## 51: **TS** ATTACKS FROM ABOVE AGAIN.

**3**

As **TS** shuffles up with his left leg, he lifts up the right stick and attempts again to poke **S** in the head as he moves into a right horse stance.

As **S** withdraws his left leg and assumes a right horse stance, he moves the spear tip from right to left and back to use the body of the spear to deflect the point of the triple stick.

Reverse view of 1

Reverse view of 3

# 52: S ATTEMPTS TO HOOK THE TRIPLE STICK AND DISARM TS.

A variety of stepping methods may be used by **S**.

METHOD 1: **S** hooks down with the butt end of the spear and does not change stance.

METHOD 2: **S** brings his left foot forward so that it is alongside the right, then he steps forward with his right leg while he hooks downward with the butt of the spear. This is done so that there is less chance of **TS** escaping.

METHOD 3: **S** may bring his right leg back to his left, and step
back again with his left foot while hooking downward with
the spear. This is done to increase the distance between **S**
and **TS**.

Depending on how you and your partner practice this set, any
of these methods are acceptable. Regardless of how **S** accomplishes his move, **TS** should be aware and step back as far as he
needs to for safety purposes and to make sure his triple stick is not
taken away.

**TS** sees this hooking motion, and so he
withdraws, bringing his right foot back to be
alongside his left foot. As he withdraws, he
keeps the triple stick up.

Reverse view of 3

# 53: THE SPEAR IS USED AS A LONG FLAIL.

Since **S** missed the opportunity to hook **TS**'s weapon, he now steps forward with his right leg and, holding the spear at the end, he attempts to strike **TS**'s head with the tip of the spear. To get more momentum in his weapon, he thrusts the butt end of the spear up while he drops his own body down, causing the spear tip to fall with greater force. **S** assumes a right side stance.

Seeing the long spear coming down upon him, **TS** withdraws his right leg and uses the middle part of the triple stick to block the spear tip. **TS** assumes a left side stance.

Reverse view of 1

Reverse view of 4

# 54: THE TRIPLE STICK THROWS OFF THE SPEAR.

TS uses the strength of his right arm to help throw the spear off the middle part of the triple stick. To do this, **TS** jerks the left stick down and back, and pushes the right stick upward with a strong right-to-left motion.

S feels his spear moving from left to right.

Reverse view of 2

# 55: THE "CROUCHING DRAGON" ATTACKS **S**'S LEGS.

After **TS** throws off the spear lying on top of the triple stick, he uses the triple stick by holding it with his right hand and whipping it in a large counterclockwise circle to strike at **S**'s legs. This is the main technique of the "crouching dragon" grip. For realism, **TS** can whip the triple stick at mid-level as shown in photo 2. For safety, **TS** can whip the triple stick along the ground as shown in the reverse view.

**S** raises up his right leg, pushes off with his left leg, and jumps over the triple stick as it comes at him from the left side. As **S** jumps up, he regains control of his spear and lands, right foot, then left foot.

Reverse view of 2

# 56: THE COILING DRAGON BLOCKS THE SPEAR.

**TS** catches the end of the triple stick with his left hand (palm up). **TS** has returned to the "coiling dragon" grip.

S thrusts the spear at **TS**'s head.

**TS** blocks the spear tip thrust by using the middle section of the triple stick. **TS** may pull back and downward with the left stick and push up and to the left side with the right stick to gain power in the block.

Reverse view of 5

# 57: THE "CROUCHING DRAGON STICK" ATTACKS FROM ABOVE.

**4**

**TS** throws the triple stick overhead directly on top of **S**'s head. He begins by simultaneously throwing the left part of the stick with his left hand, and whipping the right stick down with power. He also sinks down in his horse stance and pulls his body forward then backward to generate more force to make the stick go forward and come down hard. (Some may complete this motion by dropping into a backward leaning right side stance, while others assume a forward leaning right horse stance. Either is acceptable.) This is the "crouching dragon" grip once more.

**S** drops back into a left side stance and protects his head by using the body of the spear.

Reverse view of 4

## 58: S THRUSTS THE SPEAR AT TS'S HEAD.

**TS** pulls the triple stick back and catches it in his left hand. He is in a right cat stance and has once more assumed the "coiling dragon" grip. One of the most difficult challenges in using the triple stick is attempting to recover and control it after having unleashed it as a flail.

**S** steps up and thrusts the spear at **TS**'s head.

**TS** uses the left stick to parry the spearhead using a left-to-right motion. He pulls the right stick back in preparation for the next move.

Reverse view of 4

Reverse view of 7

# 59: THE COILING DRAGON STRIKES AT **S**'S MIDSECTION.

**5**

**TS** steps forward with his right foot, and then his left foot, into a left horse stance. At the same time, he pulls the left stick back toward himself, and thrusts the right stick forward, attempting to strike **S** in the midsection with the joint part of the triple stick.

**S** slides his right leg back, and then moves his left leg back and assumes a left cat stance. He parries the joint part of the triple stick using the body of the spear as he lifts his right hand up and moves his left hand in a left-to-right counterclockwise rising motion. Some practitioners block the triple stick using the spear part below their hands, while others use the body of the spear between their hands. Either is acceptable.

Reverse view of 5

# 60: **S**, BY EXPOSING HIS BACK, ENTICES **TS** TO ATTACK.

**3**

S attempts to bait **TS** by stepping straight back with his left leg and looking to the left over his left shoulder. He leaves the spear in full view of **TS**.

TS attempts to confuse **S** with an intricate change of hands. First, **TS** lifts his left hand over and down, and pulls his right hand back and under his left armpit. He assumes a horse stance.

Reverse view of 3

# 61: A SURPRISE ATTACK USING THE "SPLIT BEARD STICK."

As **TS** turns quickly to his right, he pushes off with his left foot, jumps up, switches stance, and lands with his right foot coming down first, followed by his left foot. (Note that alternatively **TS** could push off with his right foot, jump up, switch stance, and land with his left foot coming down first, followed by his right foot. Either is acceptable and you may do what is most comfortable for you.) Simultaneously, his left

armpit temporarily holds on to the right stick, his right hand quickly grabs the stick held in his left hand, and his left hand grabs the stick held under his left armpit. This requires a great deal of dexterity on the part of **TS**.

After **TS** finishes turning around, he attempts to strike **S**'s right leg with the right stick, although his original target was **S**'s left leg. From now until the end of the set, **TS** continues to use the "split beard" grip.

**S** sees this blow coming toward his right leg, so he continues turning toward his right, drops into a right cat stance, and thrusts the bottom of the spear downward to protect his right leg.

Reverse view of 5

Reverse view of 7

# 62: S ATTEMPTS TO STRIKE **TS** IN THE HEAD.

**3**

**S** steps into a left horse stance and attempts to strike **TS** in the back of the head with the top of the spear.

**TS** sees this strike coming, and so he blocks upward and to the right with the right stick as he assumes a right cat stance.

Reverse view of 3

# 63: S ATTEMPTS TO CUT THE BACK OF **TS**'S RIGHT LEG.

Reverse view of 2

Reverse view of 3

S, having met resistance with the block of the right stick, reverses the direction of the spear and moves it in a counterclockwise circle downward to attempt to cut the back of **TS**'s right leg. **S** uses a backward-leaning right horse stance while attempting to cut **TS**'s leg. This is done so that **S** can get more power in his movement and increase the distance so that **TS** cannot threaten him. Some wielding the spear may use a regular horse stance. Either method is acceptable.

TS lifts up his right leg to avoid being cut.

Reverse view of 4

# 64: TS STRIKES BACK AT S'S HEAD.

**TS** pushes off with his left leg, switches into a left horse stance, and strikes downward at **S**'s head with his left stick.

**S** continues with the circular motion that he had initiated earlier, by moving his spear past the lower area where **TS** formerly had his right leg. He then pulls the spear back to parry the strike of the left stick.

Reverse view of 4

Reverse view of 5

# 65: **TS** TURNS AROUND AND STRIKES AT **S**'S HEAD WITH THE RIGHT STICK.

Reverse view of 2

Reverse view of 3

Very quickly, **TS** turns to his right and assumes a right T-stance. He uses the right stick to strike down at **S**'s head. Note the similarity to the spinning backfist technique used in hand-to-hand combat.

**S** steps back with his left leg into a right horse stance and raises the spear to block the strike of the right stick with the body of the spear. The spear tip points to the left.

Reverse view of 4

## 66: **S** COUNTERATTACKS WITH AN ATTEMPTED SLAP AT **TS**'S BACK.

**5**

S brings his right foot forward, followed by his left foot, to attempt to slap **TS** in the back using the full length of the spear. This is a strong move for **S** because he can generate a great deal of power as he twists his waist clockwise and moves in with the spear using a left-to-right slapping motion. **S**'s left leg is now forward.

To protect himself, **TS** takes a step back with his left foot, then his right foot moves beside his left foot, and his left foot moves back once again. He blocks down with the right stick as he braces the triple stick against his body. His weight is 60 percent on his left leg and 40 percent on his right leg.

Reverse view of 5

## 67: **S** ATTEMPTS TO SPEAR **TS**'S HEAD.

**4**

Because **TS** is now at a distance from **S**, **S** draws the spear back with his right arm, only to shoot it forward again as he attempts to spear **TS**'s head. **S** is now in a left horse stance.

**TS** protects himself by using an "X" block. The left stick is on the inside, and he pushes the spear above his head so that the tip of the spear does not do him harm. **TS** shifts his weight forward into a right horse stance.

Reverse view of 4

## 68: **TS** ATTACKS **S**'S LEFT SHIN.

**5**

To close the gap quickly, **TS** pushes the spear upward and takes a big step forward with his left leg. He rotates his right stick in a big clockwise circle to get power, and then drops down lower so that he may strike at **S**'s leading left leg. He uses the left stick held with upward pressure to keep the spear at bay. **TS**, to gain the advantage, must try to rapidly bridge the gap with **S**.

Reverse view of 5

## 69: **S** AVOIDS THE STRIKE, JUMPS OVER, AND ATTEMPTS TO SPEAR **TS** IN THE CHEST.

**6**

To avoid the strike, **S** rears back on his right leg, lifts up his left leg, and pushing off with his right leg, jumps over the strike directed at his left leg. He lands on his left leg and immediately turns toward his left to shoot the spear forward at **TS**'s chest area. **S** is in a left horse stance. (Ideally, if **S** can turn around fast enough, he has the option of spearing **TS** in the back.)

Reverse view of 1

Reverse view of 3

After the right stick of **TS** passes under **S**'s leg, **TS** steps forward with his right leg and then immediately turns toward his left so that his back is not exposed for an undue length of time and he is not caught unawares. He uses the left stick to parry the spear thrust by quickly moving the left stick from right to left. **TS** is in a left cat stance.

Reverse view of 7

## 70:  **S** AGAIN THRUSTS THE SPEAR AT **TS**'S CHEST.

**S** advances forward and thrusts the spear again at **TS**'s chest area. **S** attempts to use his long weapon to his advantage and keep **TS** on the defensive.

**TS** steps back with his left foot and into a right cat stance. He uses the right stick to parry the spear thrust by moving the right stick from right to left.

Reverse view of 2

Reverse view of 4

## 71: **S** THRUSTS THE SPEAR AGAIN AT **TS**'S RIGHT SHIN OR KNEE.

**6**

**S** steps forward again to thrust the spear at **TS**'s right shin. **S** is in a left horse stance.

**TS**, to avoid the spear thrust to his right shin, withdraws his right leg across the front of his left leg and assumes a right T-stance. At the same time, he blocks the spear thrust by using the right stick in a downward right-to-left motion to knock the spear to the left side. **S** will feel his spear being pushed to the right side.

Reverse view of 4

Reverse view of 6

# 72: **TS** COUNTERATTACKS TO **S**'S HEAD USING A SPINNING MOTION.

**4**

While the spear of **S** is still facing downward, **TS** rapidly continues turning to the left and shifts into a left horse stance. As he moves into his left horse stance, he attempts to strike **S**'s head with the back of his left stick. Again, note the analogy to the spinning back-fist technique in hand-to-hand self-defense.

**S** shifts his weight back into a left cat stance and blocks the blow by pulling his spear back. (Some prefer to use the left cat stance as it increases the distance between **S** and **TS**. Because **S** has two hands on the spear, his block is much stronger than the single left stick of **TS**. Alternatively, some wielding the spear assume a left horse stance and then use a strong turn of the waist to accomplish this block. Either is acceptable.)

Reverse view of 3

Reverse view of 4

# 73: **S** ATTEMPTS TO CUT THE FRONT OF **TS**'S LEFT LEG.

5

To go back on the offensive, **S** moves his spear in a downward counterclockwise circle so that he can attempt to cut the front of **TS**'s left leg. Because he has two hands on the spear, he is able to force down the single left stick of **TS**.

TS feels the force of the spear so he goes with the motion of the spear and lifts up his left leg.

Reverse view of 3

Reverse view of 5

# 74: S RETURNS TO STRIKE AT THE BACK OF TS'S LEFT LEG.

**3**

After the spear passes under **TS**'s leg, **S** attempts to bring the spear back down on **TS**'s left leg. He moves the spear in a downward clockwise circle to strike at **TS**'s left leg. **S** sinks into a left cat stance.

When **TS** sees that the spear is coming back down to strike him in the back of his left leg, he moves his left stick in a complete clockwise circle to block downward to stop the spear. **TS** is in a left cat stance.

Reverse view of 3

## 75: **S** ATTACKS THE LEFT SIDE OF **TS**'S HEAD.

1

Noticing that **TS**'s head area is exposed, **S** brings his spear in an upward counterclockwise arc to strike at **TS**'s head.

    **TS** sees this strike coming and moves his left stick in a counterclockwise arc to meet the strike.

Reverse view of 2

# 76: **TS** CLOSES THE GAP AND STRIKES AT **S**'S HEAD FROM BEHIND.

Reverse view of 2

Reverse view of 4

**5**

Because **S**'s head is now exposed, **TS** uses his left stick to press down on the spear. At the same time, he steps forward with his right leg into a horse stance to use a counterclockwise motion with the right stick to strike at **S**'s head. In this last series of movements of the form, to negate the advantage of the spear's reach, **TS** continually tries to close the gap with **S** and strike him at short range. **S** will use evasive movements and strike back when opportune.

To avoid the blow, **S** quickly squats down, bends at the waist, and lowers his head.

Reverse view of 5

# 77:   S ATTEMPTS TO STRIKE TS'S RIGHT LEG AND ATTACK TS'S HEAD.

Reverse view (after figure 1 but before figure 2)        Reverse view of 2

**5**

S now uses his spear in a sweeping motion from right to left to strike or cut at **TS**'s right leg, depending on the distance and how **S** holds the spear.

**TS** sees this and lifts up his right leg quickly. However, **S** continues the motion, assumes a left horse stance, and uses a clockwise strike with the spear at **TS**'s head.

**TS** blocks this by lifting up his right stick while assuming a right cat stance.

Reverse view of 5

# 78: S ATTEMPTS TO STRIKE TS IN THE HEAD.

Reverse view (after figure 3 but before figure 4)　　　Reverse view (slightly before figure 4)

**4**

S draws back his left foot and brings up his right foot so that he assumes a right horse stance. Simultaneously, he uses the butt end of the spear in a sweeping motion from right to left.

TS shifts into a right T-stance and parries the strike of the spear using the left stick with a left-to-right sideways motion. TS does not use force against force, but instead uses his left stick to speed the spear past his own head so that he is out of danger and so that he can quickly go back on the offensive.

Reverse view of 4

## 79: **TS** GOES BACK ON THE OFFENSIVE WITH A RIGHT STICK STRIKE TO THE BACK OF **S**'S HEAD.

**4**

**TS** steps up with his left leg into a left horse stance and uses the right stick in a downward sweeping counterclockwise motion to strike **S** in the back of his head.

**S** squats down and bends at the waist to avoid the blow.

Reverse view of 3

Reverse view of 4

## 80: **S** CREATES THE DISTANCE AGAIN TO THRUST THE SPEAR AT **TS**'S HEAD.

**5**

**6**

Reverse view of 2

Reverse view of 5

**7**

**S** turns to his left, steps across his left foot with his right foot, and pivots counterclockwise. Arising, he immediately thrusts the spear at **TS**'s head. **S** is in a left horse stance.

**TS** sees the spear thrust coming and uses his left stick to block upward as he drops into a left cat stance.

Reverse view of 7

# 81: **TS** ATTACKS **S**'S HEAD AGAIN.

**5**

**TS** forces down the spear by pushing the spear to the left. He steps forward with his right leg to strike at the back of **S**'s head.

**S** squats down and bends at the waist again to avoid the blow from behind his head.

Reverse view of 2

Reverse view of 5

# 82: **S** STRIKES AT **TS**'S RIGHT LEG.

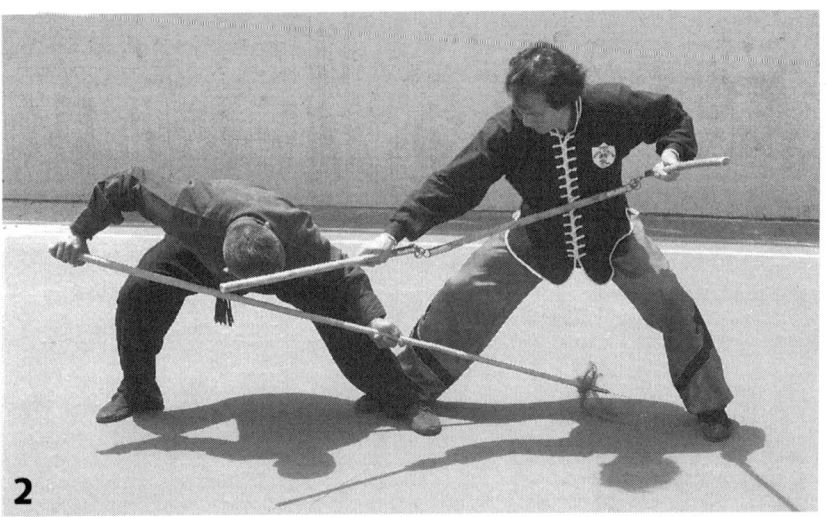

Because **S** is again in a disadvantageous position, he utilizes his spear by making a sweeping motion from right to left. With this motion he can either cut at **TS**'s leg or strike him or unbalance him.

To avoid having his leg injured, **TS** lifts up his right leg.

Reverse view of 1

Reverse view of 3

# 83: **S** CONTINUES HIS MOTION AND STRIKES AT **TS**'S HEAD.

**S** continues the motion of his spear and brings it around in a clockwise circle to strike at **TS**'s head. **S** moves into a left horse stance.

**TS** places his right foot back down on the ground after the spear has passed under it. He then blocks the spear using an upward clockwise motion with the right stick.

Reverse view of 3

## 84: **TS** ATTEMPTS A KICK AT **S**'S MIDSECTION.

Seeing that the spear tip is high, **TS** pushes off with his right leg, hops forward on his left, and attempts to kick **S** in the midsection with his right foot. **S** will shift his body back and then use his spear to parry this kick.

Reverse view of 4

## 85: **S** DOES THE FINAL PARRY.

**2**

S withdraws his right foot and assumes a left cat stance. He uses the upper end of the spear to follow the forward and upward momentum of **TS**'s right foot from underneath. By utilizing a counterclockwise circular motion with the spear, and getting power from the twisting motion of both hands, he causes **TS**'s right foot to be thrown out.

TS, feeling his right foot thrown out and to the right, follows the motion and turns to the right. The motion of **TS**'s right leg is similar to that of someone doing a lotus kick with the right leg. (This may also be considered a right leg outer crescent kick.)

Reverse view of 2

# 86: THE OPPONENTS BOTH SPIN OUT TO END THE SET.

After **S** parries **TS**'s right foot, he turns to his right and pushes off with his right leg. Continuing to turn to the right, he spins the spear tip down and then up, ending in a left cat stance.

Reverse view of 2

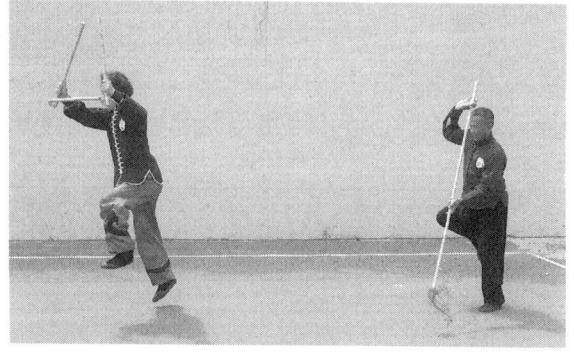

Reverse view of 5

Reverse view (after figure 5 but before figure 6)

Reverse view of 8

**9**

When **TS**'s right foot touches the ground again, he pushes off with his right foot once more, continues turning toward the right, and revolves both left and right sticks in a complete circle. When he lands, he assumes a left cat stance and crosses the sticks in an "X" pattern, right stick over the left.

Reverse view of 9

# 87: ENDING OF THE FORM.

**S** brings his left foot alongside his right foot, brings the spear back to his right side, and stands straight up.

**TS** brings his left foot alongside his right foot, separates the sticks and holds them straight out (as in the reverse-view photo), and finally folds them back inward (as in the front-view photo).

Reverse view of 1

## About North Atlantic Books

North Atlantic Books (NAB) is an independent, nonprofit publisher committed to a bold exploration of the relationships between mind, body, spirit, and nature. Founded in 1974, NAB aims to nurture a holistic view of the arts, sciences, humanities, and healing. To make a donation or to learn more about our books, authors, events, and newsletter, please visit www.northatlanticbooks.com.